Hey Kids! Let's Visit Chicago

Teresa Mills

Life Experiences Publishing

Bluff City, Tennessee

Teresa Mills/Life Experiences Publishing
PO Box 53
Bluff City, TN 37618
kid-friendly-family-vacations.com

Book Layout © 2014 BookDesignTemplates.com

Hey Kids! Let's Visit Chicago/ Teresa Mills.-1st ed.
ISBN - 978-1-946049-09-4

Contents

Preface

Welcome

Chicago is a great city to visit. The city is large, but it is very easy to get around. Like so many other places that you can visit, there are just so many things to do and see there.

This book is written as a fun fact guide about some Chicago attractions and sites. It includes some history interspersed with fun facts about things to do. The book can easily be enjoyed by younger children by reading it with them.

You can visit Chicago right from your own home! Whether you are preparing for a vacation with the family and want to learn more about the city, or just enjoy the book and pictures to learn a little more about Chicago, this book is for you.

As you continue to learn more about Chicago, I have some fun activity pages that you can download and print:

http://kid-friendly-family-vacations.com/chicagofun

When you have completed this book, I invite you to visit the other books in the series:

Hey Kids! Let's Visit Washington DC
Hey Kids! Let's Visit A Cruise Ship
Hey Kids! Let's Visit New York City
Hey Kids! Let's Visit London England
Hey Kids! Let's Visit San Francisco
Hey Kids! Let's Visit Savannah Georgia
Hey Kids! Let's Visit Paris France
Hey Kids! Let's Visit Charleston South Carolina
Hey Kids! Let's Visit Rome Italy
Hey Kids! Let's Visit Boston
Hey Kids! Let's Visit Philadelphia
Hey Kids! Let's Visit San Diego

Enjoy!

Teresa Mills

Introduction

A Little About Chicago

Chicago is situated on the shores of Lake Michigan, one of the lakes in the Great Lakes system between the United States and Canada. It was incorporated in 1837 and is now one of the most populated cities in the United States. In 1871, one third of Chicago was destroyed by fire, but the city was rebuilt very quickly.

Chicago is full of parks, museums, and tall buildings to explore. We will talk about some of the fun places to explore in this great city including Millennium Park, the Museum Campus, the Willis Tower and Skydeck, and the Lincoln Park Zoo. Chicago is also known for some iconic foods! The Chicago hotdog, the deep-dish pizza, and the Chicago blend popcorn have all helped make Chicago famous!

If you love sports, Chicago will not disappoint! Chicago is home to two major league baseball teams, an NFL football team, an NHL ice hockey team, an NBA basketball team, an MLS soccer team, a WNBA basketball team, and a NWSL soccer team! So, you should get your fill of sports no matter the time of year!

So, are you ready?

Let's Visit Chicago!

1

Art Institute of Chicago

The Art Institute of Chicago (AIC) was founded in 1879, which makes it one of the oldest art museums in the United States. It is also one of the largest art museums, being home to around 300,000 works of many great artists such as Pablo Picasso, Vincent van Gogh, Claude Monet, and Edward Hopper.

In 2009, the AIC opened a new wing designed by Renzo Piano called the "Modern Wing." This new area of the museum extended the structure to nearly one million square feet. That's about as big as six football fields! Because of this incredible development, the AIC became the second-largest art museum in the United States, next to the Metropolitan Museum of Art in New York.

Before it was called the Art Institute, it was first named the Chicago Academy of Design. It was built in 1866 by 35 artists who wanted to create a school that had its own room where art can be displayed. Because many students wanted to learn the arts and become artists, the Chicago Academy of Design was able to open a five-story building that became their school and art gallery.

In 1871, the building was destroyed during the Great Chicago Fire. Because of this, they lost all their money and had no means to maintain the school. To save the school, an organization bought what remained of the school and renamed it as the Chicago Academy of Fine Arts. It was finally given the name Art Institute of Chicago in 1882.

Charles L. Hutchinson, a banker and philanthropist (a person who gives generously in order to help others), was elected as its first president. Many people consider Mr. Hutchinson as the person who greatly helped in developing the Art Institute of Chicago to what it is today.

Art Institute of Chicago Lion

Currently, more than 300,000 masterpieces are housed in the 11 different departments in the Art Institute:

- Indian Art of the Americas and African Art
- American Art
- Ancient and Byzantine
- Architecture and Design
- Asian Art
- European Decorative Arts
- European Paintings and Sculpture
- Modern and Contemporary Art
- Photography
- Prints and Drawings
- Textiles

Some great works by famous artists that can be found in the AIC are El Greco's *Saint Martin and the Beggar*, Eugene Delacroix's *The Combat of the Giaour and Hassan*, Vincent van Gogh's *Self-portrait*, Claude Monet's *Water Lilies*, Pablo Picasso's *Head of a Woman*, and Grant Wood's *American Gothic*.

Fun facts about the Art Institute of Chicago:

- Two bronze lions guard the main entrance to the museum. These lions are not identical and actually have unofficial names: "On the Prowl" and "Stands in the Attitude of Defiance."

- When one of the Chicago sports teams plays in a championship tournament (for instance the Super Bowl or the Stanley Cup Finals), the lions sometimes dress in the team uniform.
- The artist of the largest painting in the museum, Georgia O' Keeffe, was a student at the Art Institute of Chicago. The painting is entitled *The Sky Above the Clouds IV* and is 24 feet long and 8 feet high!

2

Chicago Cultural Center

One of Chicago's most famous landmarks, the Chicago Cultural Center (CCC), is located at the Chicago Loop (a busy section of the city where many museums and iconic attractions are located) across Michigan Avenue coming from Millennium Park. It was first opened in 1897 and is operated by the Department of Cultural Affairs and Special Events.

The Cultural Center was first built as Chicago's central library building. In 1977, it was transformed into a culture and art center through the initiative of the Cultural Affairs Commissioner Lois Weisberg. Hundreds of events, programs, and showcases are held at the CCC each year, where hundreds and thousands of tourists and visitors come to watch.

A group of architects named Shepley, Rutan, and Coolidge designed this famous building which was first intended to be a central library, a meeting hall, and a memorial for an organization called the Grand Army of the Republic. It has two wings: the North Wing has 4 stories and the South Wing has 5 stories.

The world's largest stained-glass Tiffany dome can be found at the building's South Wing. It measures 38 feet from one side to the other and was made using 30,000 pieces of stained glass. Meanwhile, the North Wing features another dome with a diameter of 40 feet, having 50,000 pieces of stained glass. This dome features a beautiful Renaissance (a period in history when arts and politics were reborn) pattern designed by Healy & Millet.

Tourists not only come for the events held in the CCC but also to appreciate the amazing architecture. Aside from the two glass domes, people also visit the CCC to observe the entrance on Randolph Street with its majestic columns, artistic wooden doors, detailed ceiling, and walls that are made of marble. At the Washington Street entrance, people can see big bronze doors and a grand staircase made from different colored marble stones. It is also designed with many colorful glass tiles that make up a beautiful mosaic pattern.

Staircase in Chicago Cultural Center

In 2017, an artist named Kerry James Marshall was asked to create a mural on the west side of the building. The mural featured many artists who had a big contribution to the culture of Chicago like TV personality Oprah Winfrey, poet Gwendolyn Brooks, and writer Sandra Cisneros.

Fun facts about the Chicago Cultural Center:

- Free public events are held at the CCC where visitors can watch art exhibits, dance, music, and theater performances.
- The Chicago Cultural Center is the official place where the Mayor of Chicago greets very important people who come to visit the

city like presidents, government officials, and royalties.

- The Chicago Children's Choir's headquarters is located in this building.

3

Harold Washington Library

Named after the first African American city mayor of Chicago, the Harold Washington Library is the central library for the Chicago Public Library System. It is located at 400 S. State Street, along the southern part of Chicago's Loop.

After the old central library was transformed into the Chicago Cultural Center, most of the library's collections were stored while waiting for a new library. When Harold Washington became mayor, he supported the construction of a new central library. A contest was held to determine the design of the new library. It was won by architects Hammond, Beeby, and Babcka.

The library was officially opened on October 7, 1991. Richard M. Daley, who was the new mayor when the library was opened, named it after the previous mayor to honor his initiative and support for the completion of the library. The models that the architects used in designing the library are displayed on the building's eighth floor today.

The Harold Washington Library is also known for its beautiful architecture. Tourists who come to Chicago often visit the library to admire its amazing designs both outside and inside the building. Its exterior has a similar style with other buildings along the Loop like the Rookery, the Auditorium, and the Monadnock. Detailed metal ornaments called acroteria were added to the building's roof in 1993.

Harold Washington Library

Facing State Street is an acroterium (an architectural ornament attached to the corner of a building) of an owl, the symbol of wisdom, and the Greek goddess Athena. On Ida B. Wells Drive, there are seed pods that depict the bountiful harvest in the Midwest.

Beautiful granite blocks make up the library's face together with an iconic red brick wall. Dividing the two portions are wall medallions of Ceres, the Roman goddess of agriculture, together with ears of corn. Of course, the front of the building is just one part of its exceptional beauty because the other parts of the building feature windows that are five stories high!

The library is located near schools and universities like Columbia College, Robert Morris College, Roosevelt University, and DePaul University, so many students come here to study and do schoolwork. The library also has an auditorium, a multi-purpose room, and an exhibit hall. It offers different services like 3D printing and laser cutting for a minimal fee. Some sections can cater to the blind, visually impaired, and physically disabled.

Fun facts about the Harold Washington Library:

- You can find a winter-garden roof penthouse in the Harold Washington Library.
- The Pritzker family, one of Chicago's wealthiest families, supported the construction of the building together with Mayor Harold Washington.
- All of the public doors of the library lead to the lobby.
- There are five enormous aluminum owl statues perched on the corners of the library roof. The owls represent wisdom.

4

Lakefront Trail

Chicago's Lakefront Trail is a path that extends for 18 miles along Lake Michigan on Chicago's eastern side.

The trail was first designated as Chicago's official bike path. As more people used the trail, the local government of Chicago, through the Trail Separation Project, improved and added a path for non-biking pedestrians.

Another improvement made on the Lakefront trail was the construction of a Navy Pier Flyover, which goes over the Chicago River. The bridge extends from the north side of Ohio Street Beach, ending at Navy Pier and DuSable Park. Construction of the bridge began in 2014 and was recently completed in May 2021.

Visitors can enjoy several different activities on the trail like walking, running, biking, and skating. People living in Chicago use the trail to get to work, train for marathons, or just for a relaxing walk.

Lakefront trail

If you walk along the Lakefront Trail, you will pass many cultural and tourist attractions. The trail begins 9.5 miles south of downtown Chicago at South Shore Cultural Center. From there, you will pass Jackson Park, the Museum of Science and Industry, and Promontory Point. Promontory Point is a peninsula, a body of land extending toward the water. That's why this place gives you a unique view of the Chicago skyline.

Chicago Skyline

Further along the path, you will pass Burnham Park, which has some natural sanctuaries. There is also Adler Planetarium and Shedd Aquarium, which is located right by the middle of the city of Chicago. As you go along, you will reach Lincoln Park that is a one-stop destination as it is home to a nature museum, a zoo, and an observatory. It is right across from North Avenue Beach, one of Chicago's most popular beaches.

Because a lot of people often come to enjoy traveling down the trail, accessing the trail is very easy. There are restrooms, restaurants, souvenir shops, and even a carnival for people to enjoy their experience at Lakefront Trail. The trail is also pet-friendly and has several dog parks so that the whole family can have a fun and relaxing time in Chicago.

Fun facts about the Lakefront Trail:

- Lakefront Trail goes through several beaches, namely South Shore Beach, Ohio Street Beach, Oak Street Beach, North Avenue Beach, Montrose Beach, and Foster Beach.
- Because of its length and various attractions, the trail welcomes more than 30,000 people every day.

- A man named Aaron Montgomery Ward prevented any person or company that tried to construct a building on the lakefront. Because of his efforts, the lakefront maintains a pure and natural view of the lake.

5

Maggie Daley Park

Maggie Daley Park is one of the best local parks in Chicago. It used to be an old parking lot and a sunken rail yard! In the mid-1970s, it was called the Richard J. Daley Bicentennial Plaza to honor Chicago's former mayor, Richard J. Daley (1902-1976). Back then, it was an underground parking garage with outdoor recreational facilities.

In 2009, the City of Chicago and the Park District slowly began to transform it into the park it is today. It took several years of planning. Many citizens joined in and pitched their thoughts into how the park can best serve the city. The Park District also hired an international architecture firm, Michael Van Valkenburgh Associates to design the park.

The park was later renamed Maggie Daley Park, in honor of Maggie C. Daley (1943-2011) who was

Chicago's first lady. She made deep contributions in helping children and was the co-founder of Gallery 37, a summer art program for teens in Chicago. She is also responsible for starting After School Matters. It is a non-profit organization for Chicago teenagers that presents innovative out-of-school activities.

With the transformation came lots of things to do and see at Maggie Daley Park. You can explore the play garden, discover the picnic groves, play on the tennis courts, have fun with the mini-golf course, or test your skills on the rock climbing wall!

Maggie Daley Park is located within the Chicago Loop (The Loop is a busy section of the city where many museums and iconic attractions are located). You can access the park either by public transportation or by car with nearby parking options to choose from. Bike parking is also available. However, bike riding inside the park is against park rules. It is encouraged to park your bikes and leave them in the designated area before heading into the park.

Maggie Daley Park

Fun Facts about Maggie Daley Park:

- Maggie Daley Park has a dog access path for dog lovers and pet owners.
- The architecture firm Michael Van Valken-burgh Associates designed the park with curvilinear (a design bounded by curved lines) pathways so visitors can see many landscapes the park can offer as they walk through the site.
- Maggie Daley Park is a 20-acre park worth about $55 million. It officially opened on December 13, 2014.

6

Willis Tower – Sky Deck

A 110-story building, Willis Tower and Skydeck is an iconic tower. It is one of the tallest buildings in Chicago. Willis Tower is a tall building with great views of Chicago with lots of fun and exciting things to do.

On the Skydeck, you will get a breathtaking 360-degree view of the city. With a view extending 50 miles in all directions, you can see the states of Illinois, Michigan, Indiana, and Wisconsin all from the same floor. To enter the tower, you will need to pay for the general admissions ticket. Online tickets are offered as well.

If you are brave enough, try stepping onto the Ledge and look down! From a height of 1,353 feet, you will get a clear view of the city under your feet.

From top to bottom, the ledge is made out of glass material, giving you a unique unforgettable experience.

Willis Tower Skydeck Ledge

Be sure to take some cool photos while standing inside the Ledge, and maybe even tray some stunts. The Ledge is designed to hold 10,000 lbs. and endure 5 tons of pressure. Just be prepared to wait your turn getting into the glass deck. Each visitor usually takes 2-3 minutes on the Ledge so more people can get their turn.

The iconic tower has a lobby full of interactive exhibits and interesting trivia that highlights the
Windy City. There are plenty of activities to do,
and there is even a section just for kids. To make
their day special, Willis Tower offers fun interactive
activities like scavenger hunts, coloring pages, and
interesting fact sheets.

Formerly known as Sears Tower, Willis Tower is a
short walk from Union Station. It is also accessible
with the new Jackson Boulevard entrance. Nearby
is the famous Catalog, a 5-level urban destination
with several restaurants, specialty stores, and entertainment facilities. This is a great place to
explore during your vacation.

**Fun facts about the Willis Tower and Sky-
deck:**

- Willis Tower has a height of 1,450 feet (443
  meters). That makes it one of the tallest
  towers in the United States.
- Each year, the Skydeck receives approximately 1.7 million visitors. That's a lot!
- The Ledge's glass box has a 4.3-foot exten-
  sion from the Skydeck building. It can
  retract into the building to make it easier to
  clean.

7

Hancock 360 Chicago Observatory

The Hancock 360 Chicago Observatory is on the 94th floor of a 100-story building. It offers a spectacular view of Lake Michigan and a 360-degree view of the Windy City. You can even see Willis Tower, with its two iconic antennas over the skyline. The 360 Chicago is located on Michigan Avenue, right beside Lake Michigan.

One of the main highlights of the Hancock 360 Observation deck is the Tilt. It is a thrilling ride where you tilt at a 30-degree angle out of the building with nothing but glass between you and 1,000 feet (305 meters) from the ground. There are 8 glass windows. Each is equipped with steel handrails to hold on to while tilting down, giving you an adrenaline rush.

All visitors must purchase a general admissions ticket to enter the observatory. It includes free access to the Skywalk, the observation deck, the Bar 94, and access to their interactive touchscreens. Children ages 3 and below have free admission to enter the Hancock 360 Chicago Observatory. To experience the Tilt, you need to purchase separate tickets.

View from Hancock 360 Chicago Observatory

Compared to Willis Tower, 360 Chicago has smaller crowds and shorter waiting hours. It also has a unique souvenir shop and a small bar where you can sit and enjoy the view. There are online activities for kids to do while exploring 360

Chicago, including an interactive display to learn more about Chicago's rich culture.

The Hancock 360 Chicago Observatory is conveniently located near the Magnificent Mile District, famous for its shops and restaurants.

Fun facts about the Hancock 360 Chicago Observatory:

- The Hancock 360 Chicago Observatory was first opened in 1969.
- The 360 Chicago elevators are among the fastest in the country. They can travel approximately 20 miles/hour.
- Not only can you see a view of Lake Michigan and the city skyline in Chicago, but you can also see 4 neighboring states (Illinois, Indiana, Wisconsin, and Michigan).
- The Tilt meets the highest safety standards and is inspected regularly.

8

Tribune Tower

The Tribune Tower is a popular architectural gem standing at 435 North Michigan Avenue in Chicago. Its construction started in 1923 and was completed in 1925.

The Tribune Tower is the crowning jewel of the 75th-anniversary celebration of the city's premier daily newspaper, the Chicago Tribune. The journalists behind the newspaper launched an international competition that sought the "most beautiful building in the world."

Over 260 architectural designs were submitted from 23 different countries. The design of Raymond M. Hood and John Mead Howells was selected as the winner. In addition to winning the prize money amounting to $100,000, their design was brought to life as the Tribune Tower. It became the main headquarters of Tribune

Publishing, including the Chicago Tribune and Tribune Media.

Tribune Tower

The Tribune Tower served as the "cathedral of journalism." It was home to the city's premier journalists and press corps. Secondly, the architectural design and structure of the tower adopted a neo-gothic style known as the architectural movement which inspired many European churches since the 17th century. Many architects also say that the tower is a culmination of past architectural ideas such as the "American Perpendicular System" and "Butter Tower."

The most unique feature of the Tribune Tower is that it features some parts, stones, or fragments of many historical sites and architectural gems all over the world. These parts were integrated into the tower structure itself. To honor these treasures, each stone or brick is properly labeled corresponding to their origins.

Some of these featured sites are:

- Taj Mahal
- The Parthenon
- Great Wall of China
- Berlin Wall
- Great Pyramid
- Corregidor Island
- Westminster Palace
- St. Stephen's Cathedral

- Clementine Hall
- Abraham Lincoln's Tomb
- Fort Santiago
- Ta Phrom
- Rouen Cathedral
- Notre Dame de Paris
- Angkor Wat

The Tribune Tower also has influence in popular culture. It was featured in many movies and TV shows like *Crime Scene Investigation: New York*, *The Tonight Show with Conan O'Brien*, *One Wedding and a Funeral*, and *Transformers: Dark of the Moon*.

Fun Facts about the Tribune Tower:

- The Tribune Tower received a moon rock from Buzz Aldrin during the 30th anniversary commemoration of the Apollo 13 mission.
- The tower received a piece of steel from the World Trade Center after the devastating 9-11 bombing.
- The total height of Tribune Tower including the antenna is approximately 496 feet.

9

Grant Park

Grant Park, or "Chicago's Front Yard," is located in the Loop area of Chicago, a busy section of the city where many museums and iconic attractions are located. It is considered the heart of community affairs and home to many iconic landmarks of Chicago.

Grant Park has very early beginnings. In 1844, the city government designated the vacant land found in the eastern region of the Michigan River as Chicago's official park. It was originally named the Lake Park. Due to events in history like the construction of the Illinois Central Railroad and the Great Chicago Fire, the park was pushed further towards Lake Michigan. Subsequent land reclamations initiated by the government expanded the total park area so it now measures approximately 319 acres. After the American Civil War, the park was renamed Grant Park in honor of U.S. President Ulysses Grant.

All through the park's long history, it has been part of many monumental events. The funeral procession of late President Abraham Lincoln as well as Pope John Paul's 1979 outdoor mass were held in the park. Grant Park was also where Barack Obama celebrated his successful presidential election in 2008.

Fountain in Grant Park

In addition to the park's historical significance, it also houses many of the city's iconic landmarks. One of which is the world-renowned Art Institute of Chicago. On top of being one of the best art schools on the entire continent, the art institute also houses more than 300,000 art works gathered from all over the world.

Grant Park celebrates both history and art. It is where the great Millennium Park is situated and where Jay Pritzker Pavilion and Cloud Gate are found. These sites have witnessed many world-class performances by artists from all over the world. Grant Park also houses the following iconic landmarks:

- Abraham Lincoln: The Head of State statue
- Columbus monument
- General Logan monument
- The Agora
- Buckingham Fountain
- Congress Plaza
- Children's Museum

Fun Facts about Grant Park:

- Buckingham Fountain, found in the center of Grant Park, is the 7th largest man-made fountain in the world.
- Grant Park has a marina named "The Queen's Landing" in honor of Queen Elizabeth's visit in 1959 aboard the Royal Yacht Britannia.

- Grant Park has staged numerous musical festivals including the Lollapalooza.

10

Chicago Museum Campus

The Chicago Museum Campus is a museum park with an area of approximately 57 acres. It is located near Grant Park and showcases some of Chicago's most iconic attractions: the Shedd Aquarium, the Adler Planetarium, and the Field Museum. So, with just one stop at the Museum Campus, you can learn about world cultures and history at the Field Museum, interact with and watch aquatic animals at the Shedd Aquarium, and explore outer space and galaxies at the Alder Planetarium.

Adler Planetarium

The Adler Planetarium is a museum mainly focusing on astrophysics and astronomy. It was founded in 1930 by a Chicago businessman named

Max Adler. The planetarium was launched and opened to the public in 1930, and it was designated as a National Historic Landmark in 1987.

You will find an enormous collection of antique scientific instruments and print materials in the Adler Planetarium. The planetarium also has three full-size theaters, a space capsule, and space science exhibitions that space lovers will enjoy.

The Adler Planetarium also has outdoor sculptures such as *Spiral Galaxy* by John David Mooney, *America's Courtyard* by Ary Perez and Denise Milan, and *Man Enters the Cosmos* by Henry Moore.

Watching a show in the theater is an adventure where you will take a look into space and explore planets, stars, and galaxies. You can also visit the Mission Moon exhibit and launch a stomp rocket. A visit to the Our Solar System exhibit will allow you to examine and touch a moon rock or a meteorite. Before you finish exploring, be sure to take a peek inside the Gemini 12 spacecraft.

Adler Planetarium

Shedd Aquarium

Shedd Aquarium is a 5-million U.S. gallon indoor aquarium in Chicago. It opened on May 30, 1930, and it is one of the world's largest indoor facilities.

It has approximately 32,000 aquatic animals including sharks, amphibians, sea turtles, and rays.

Shedd Aquarium was declared a National Historic Landmark in 1987 and was the first inland aquarium to house a saltwater fish collection. The Association of Zoos and Aquariums recognized it as the "best exhibit" for Seahorse Symphony in

1999, Amazon Rising in 2001, and Wild Reef in 2004.

You can visit the underwater viewing gallery and see the dolphins zip through the water. You will be amazed watching a smiling beluga whale face-to-face. You can also go to the Polar Play Zone, dress up as penguins, and discover ice caves and the aquatic world.

Shedd Aquarium

Field Museum

The Field Museum is popular for the quality and size of its scientific and educational programs, as well as artifact collections and extensive scientific specimens. It is one of the largest national history museums in the world.

The 1893 World's Columbian Exposition and the artifacts on display inspired the creation of the Field Museum. Edward Ayer persuaded the merchant Marshall Field to help finance the establishment of the museum to accommodate the collections and artifacts for future generations.

The museum was originally named the Columbian Museum of Chicago, but its name was changed into Field Museum of Natural History in 1905.

You can learn more about natural history at the Field Museum's exhibits. You can see Maximo the Titanosaur, the largest dinosaur that lived on earth, in the Stanley Field Hall of the museum.

You can also go to the Evolving Planet exhibit where you can see a great collection of prehistoric fossils of various organisms and dinosaurs. Then head to the Underground Adventure where you will meet a wolf spider and a giant mole cricket.

Field Museum

11

Chicago Riverwalk

Chicago Riverwalk is a downtown waterfront park with walking paths. The Riverwalk is found along the main branch of the Chicago River, crossing Lakes Shore Drive, Michigan, and Lake Street.

Older generations have a different memory of the Chicago Riverwalk. Before its development, the shoreline served as the main point of the city's industrial shipping and sewer system. The growing economy and booming population of the city additionally polluted the waters of the Chicago River. The murky-colored water and its bad smell offended locals and tourists alike.

The government spent a lot of time and effort cleaning the water of the Chicago River. The first initiative to rehabilitate the dying river was done in 1900 when the natural water flow of the river was reversed. This ambitious project was made possible through civil engineering. The government, in partnership with other private organizations, then began more rehabilitation projects for the river. In 2001, the Chicago Department of Transportation implemented the reconstruction project of Wacker Drive which led to the formal construction and development of the Chicago Riverwalk.

Chicago Riverwalk

The improvements in the quality of the Chicago River water opened a lot of opportunities for tourism. The development of the Riverwalk was spearheaded by three notable architects: Skidmore, Owings, and Merrill. They divided the entire stretch into four main districts: Confluence,

Arcade, Civic, and Market. These districts were recently converted into rooms. Currently, the Chicago Riverwalk has six major rooms.

Each room houses several establishments like restaurants, bars, cafés, gardens, ports, and parks. Among the first settlers at the Riverwalk was the Chicago Architecture Foundation River Cruise. They have been in service for 25 years now and are considered one of the best boat tours in Northern America. It has a unique route that tours the passengers along the river while introducing the buildings with remarkable architectural designs.

Some of the most visited recreational and historical spaces along the Chicago River are:

- Vietnam Veterans Memorial Plaza
- River Theater
- McCormick Bridgehouse and Chicago River Museum
- Floating Garden
- Centennial Fountain

Chicago River

Fun Facts About Chicago Riverwalk:

- The water reversal project of Chicago drew a lot of controversies and legal battles. Chicago's neighbors in the south, especially Missouri, were not happy with the idea.
- The diversion of the water faced ecological problems such as the invasion of Asian Carp fish.
- The government spent millions of U.S. dollars to redefine the channel systems and to revamp the once-forgotten shoreline.

12

Navy Pier

The Navy Pier, located in the Streeterville community, features the shorelines of Lake Michigan and is one of Chicago's most visited tourist attractions. According to records, the pier entertains at least 2 million people every year.

Through its history, this 14-hectare (34.59 acres) area of land was used for multiple purposes before it was transformed into what it is today. In its beginnings, around 1916 it was named the Municipal Pier. During this time, the pier served as a dock for freights and passengers.

By the year 1927, the pier was renamed Navy Pier in honor of World War I veterans. In World War II, the Navy Pier became a massive training ground for the U.S. Navy. Historical accounts state that there could have been more than 10,000 soldiers and staff who took shelter at Navy Pier during the war.

The pier was left unused and stagnant until 1995 when major redevelopment plans were started. One of the biggest changes in the pier was its cultural and entertainment spaces.

Aerial View of the Navy Pier

Today, Navy Pier is known for its celebration of art, culture, cuisine, and tradition. It has hosted several art exhibits through the years and staged more than 650 performances of world-class artists. The Pier is also home to many recreational sites like the following:

- Children's Museum
- Crystal Garden
- Chicago's Funhouse Maze

- Chicago Shakespeare Theater
- Polk Bros Park
- East End Plaza
- Fifth Third Bank Family Pavilion

The Navy Pier is also known for their summer fireworks that take place between Memorial and Labor Day.

Fun Facts About the Navy Pier:

- The most iconic landmark at Navy Pier is its Ferris Wheel called the Centennial Wheel. The original wheel was installed in 1995 and retired in 2015. The current Centennial Wheel stands 200 feet from the ground, equipped with climate-controlled gondolas.
- In the 2014 movie *Divergent*, the scene "Capture the Flag" was heavily inspired by Navy Pier, especially by the Children's Museum and Centennial Wheel.
- The pier houses the world-famous Shakespeare theater that showcases numerous plays, musicals, and films based on the works of the great playwright.

13

Garfield Park Conservatory

Chicago's Garfield Park Conservatory is a 184-acre conservatory that houses hundreds of plant species, numerous ecosystems, and marvelous landscapes. Since its establishment in 1908, the conservatory remains committed to its mission of bringing people closer to nature.

Garfield Park Conservatory started construction around 1906 headed by Jens Jensen. During his time, the idea of cultivating landscapes in an enclosed glass-made structure was revolutionary. He needed all the help he could get from engineers, architects, sculptors, and artisans to make the conservatory a reality.

The conservatory had to overcome several hurdles before it became what it is today. The management had so little support that plant culti-vation and maintenance were severely challenged. Then in 1994, a private organization funded the multimillion-dollar restoration and rehabilitation of the conservatory. In 2011, the conservatory faced a tragic loss of numerous rooms to a catastrophic hailstorm. It several years for the damaged show-rooms to re-open to the public.

Even after a century has passed, the Garfield Park Conservatory still follows the original principles of Jensen when he created it. These are illuminated by the existing rooms found inside the Garfield Park Conservatory.

Garfield Park Conservatory

One of the conservatory's notable rooms is the Desert Room. The room was designed to re-enact the harsh and dry conditions of the desert where special plants called succulents survive and thrive. Inside, you will see some of the most unique species of succulents and cacti gathered from all around the world.

The Garfield Park Conservatory also cultivates huge palm trees that can measure approximately 65 feet vertically. These plants are currently housed in the Palm Room. Up until 2012, the Palm Room was the habitat of a rare palm species called double coconut palm, an endemic species to Seychelles in East Africa. Double coconut palms bear the largest plant seed in the world. However, after 57 years since its arrival at the conservatory, the palm died of unknown causes.

The Garfield Park Conservatory has received multiple awards celebrating its significance and contribution to society. It won the 2012 National Medal for Museum and Library Services, while in 2018 it was tagged under the Illinois 200 Great Places by the American Institute of Architects.

Other than the desert and palm room, the Garfield Park Conservatory also houses the following showrooms and natural landscapes:

- Fern Room
- Sugar from the Sun
- Aroid House
- Children's Garden
- Horticultural Hall
- Artist's Garden
- Sensory Garden
- City Garden
- Demonstration Garden
- Play and Grow Garden

Fun Facts About the Garfield Conservatory:

- Garfield Park Conservatory is better known as the "landscape art under the glass" for combining the art of nature and structure.
- It took the conservatory several years to repair the damages of the 2011 hailstorm.
- The conservatory is like a seed that started small. The revolutionary idea is now a well-recognized horticultural facility in the world.

14

Museum of Science and Industry

The Chicago Museum of Science and Industry is a science and technology museum found in Jackson Park, near Lake Michigan and the University of Chicago.

The Museum of Science and Industry has a very rich and deep history. Its early beginning started in 1893 when it was still called the Palace of Fine Arts. During this time, the museum collected and showcased works of art gathered from all over the world. The art museum soon evolved into the Field Museum of Natural History which then moved to a new location as the Chicago Field Museum. This museum building then became a science museum and was named the Museum of Science and Industry.

The establishment of the museum was spear-headed by a philanthropist named Julius Rosenwald. In addition to financing the project, he also got the help of many curators and experts to find and collect pieces for the museum. The combined efforts over the past century have helped the museum grow into what it is today – a 400,000 square feet home of history and science.

Today, the museum features many exhibits staged in over 75 halls. The museum's exhibits cover everything under the sun including biology, science inventions, history, and even entertainment.

Chicago Museum of Science and Industry

One of the museum's most-visited exhibits is the "Genetics and Baby Chick Hatchery" where its visitors can learn the genetic code of life. The museum also has state-of-the-art models of the human body that explain how it functions and operates.

But the greatest pride of MSI lies in their technology and innovation exhibits. They have on display a real German submarine captured during World War II called the German Submarine U-505. They also have America's first diesel-electric passenger train named Pioneer Zephyr.

On top of all these, the museum also stages the following exhibits:

- Henry Crown Space Center
- Farm Tech
- Transportation Gallery
- Mirror Maze
- Science Storms
- ToyMaker 3000
- Coal Mine
- Yesterday's Main Street
- Art of the Bicycle
- Christmas Around the World and Holidays of Light (November – January)

Fun Facts About the Museum of Science and Industry:

- MSI welcomed the traveling exhibitions of many popular movies such as Harry Potter, Titanic, and Star Wars.
- The museum has an Omnimax theater with a giant screen.
- Based on estimates, the museum is in possession of over 3,500 artifacts.

15

Lincoln Park Zoo

Lincoln Park Zoo is the city's center of wildlife. The 35-acre zoo is home to approximately 1,100 animals of 200 unique species.

Based on historical records, Lincoln Park Zoo was established around the 18th century through the efforts of Lincoln Park and Central Park Commissioners. Its first animals were a pair of swans, 8 peacocks, 2 elks, 3 wolves, 4 eagles, and a puma. The zoo also served as a home to the critically extinct American Bison, which was later released into the wild to contribute to its species breeding and conservation program.

Since its establishment, the Lincoln Park Zoo has developed and expanded tremendously. One of the notable exhibits is the Walter Family Arctic Tundra which houses a polar bear. The zoo also has African penguins in captivity, which are housed in Robert and Mayari Pritzker Penguin Cove.

Lincoln Park Zoo has also dedicated a lot of effort to collecting and taking care of the world's most beautiful primates. Inside the zoo's Helen Brach Primate House are the black howler monkeys, Francois langur, black and white colobus, pied tamarins, and northern white-cheeked gibbons. The more unique Japanese macaques are housed in the Regenstein Macaque Forest. In 2003, a crowned lemur was added to the zoo's primate exhibit.

Lincoln Park Zoo

Several bird species, ranging from the docile to the most vicious are also found in the zoo. The zoo has the proud American bald eagles and strong cinereous vultures. They also showcase the Chilean flamingo, Palawan peacock pheasant, Puerto Rican Parrot, and several others.

The Lincoln Park Zoo completes its collection of diverse species of reptiles and amphibians including the rare axolotls, green tree python, rattlesnake, and poison dart frogs.

Some of the major exhibits housed by Lincoln Park Zoo are:

- Regenstein African Journey – Rhinoceros, African Elephants, Meerkats, Dwarf Crocodiles, Gazelles
- Regenstein Center for African Apes – Lowland Gorillas, Chimpanzees
- Pritzker Family Children's Zoo – Otters, Duck, Wolf, Bear
- Kovler Seal Pool
- Antelope & Zebra Area

Fun Facts about the Lincoln Park Zoo:

- Lincoln Park Zoo is the fourth oldest zoo in North America.
- Even a century after its opening, the Lincoln Park Zoo remains free of charge.
- A Viking Ship used to be located in the zoo. It was removed in 1994.

16

Chicago History Museum

The Chicago History Museum, located at 1601 North Clark Street of Lincoln Park, is Chicago's oldest cultural institution.

The museum was founded in 1856 and first named the Chicago Historical Society. Originally, its purpose was to research and interpret Chicago's rich history. In 1871, the Chicago Historical Society and most of their historical artifacts were destroyed in the Great Chicago Fire. Then 3 years later, in 1874, another fire in the museum broke out, which burned the remaining collection into ashes.

It took the curators and management almost 25 years to re-open and to make the collection available for public viewing. The acquisition of historical pieces linked to the American Civil War and

Abraham Lincoln have transformed it into a true public museum. In 2006, the museum formally changed its name to Chicago Historical Museum.

One of the most researched and well-curated exhibits inside the Chicago Historical Museum is the Abraham Lincoln exhibit. It explores the events during the election of Lincoln, his leadership during the Civil War, and the depressing event of his assassination. In a separate exhibit, CHM also features the relationship of Abraham Lincoln to the city of Chicago. According to historical accounts, the city served as a second home and a political stronghold of the late president.

The Chicago History Museum also houses an impressive collection of materials related to Chicago's local history. The curators have collected and preserved numerous research materials like publications, books, manuscripts, paintings, and photos related to the city of Chicago. The museum features a film entitled "The Great Chicago Adventure Film" in its very own in-house theater. The movie travels through time and reminisces some of the most memorable and critical points of local history including the Great Chicago Fire up to Barrack Obama's victory speech in Grant Park.

Through the course of the museum's service, it has held many iconic exhibits such as:

- American Liberty
- Works and Life of Martin Luther King
- Chicago: Crossroads of America
- Sensing Chicago
- Facing Freedom in America

Fun Facts About the Chicago History Museum:

- Due to two consecutive fires that the Chicago Historical Society experienced in the past, the current Chicago History Museum building was constructed using fire-proof materials.
- One of the most precious historical artifacts destroyed in the fire was Lincoln's final draft of the Emancipation Proclamation.
- The first passenger car from the Chicago 'L' is housed in the museum.

17

Millennium Park

Millennium Park used to be an old railroad track and parking lot. Mayor Richard Daley wanted to take this plot of land and turn it into a public green space. It was his ambition to make Chicago one of the most culturally-rich and greenest cities in North America. Now, Millennium Park is a public garden surrounded by sculptures and art galleries.

Before the park was created, the land was in use by the Illinois Central Railroad (ICR). The city filed a case against the railroad pointing out that the company was no longer using the property for railroad purposes, making the original 1852 contract with the city invalid. They won the case. The ICR had to hand over the property to the city. By claiming the property rights of the land, Daley's dream of turning it into a public green space came true.

As a world-class park, Millennium Park provides free cultural programs. Visit the crown fountain. Watch free shows in the Jay Pritzker Pavilion. Take a sightseeing tour in the Lurie garden. Explore the gardens of Millennium Park. Visit the Millennium Monument at Wrigley Square. There are tons of fun things to do at Millennium Park.

Jay Pritzker Pavilion

One of the park's main highlights is the Cloud Gate, also nicknamed The Bean. It is a 12-foot high structure which weighs 110 tons. Created by Anish Kapoor, taking inspiration from liquid mercury, he gave it a stainless steel skin. It reflects Chicago's everyday activities and a clear view of the city's skyline. What is even more amazing is the Bean's ability to expand and contract, depending on Chicago's weather conditions.

Cloud Gate

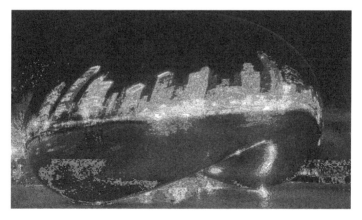

Cloud Gate at Night with Skyline Reflection

Millennium Park is free to enter for the general public. Pets are not allowed in the park; only service animals are allowed. You can bring your food and beverages into the park. Concessions are available and located on the McCormick Tribune Plaza. Millennium Park is located within Chicago's loop community.

Fun Facts About Millennium Park

- Millennium Park receives approximately 20 million visitors each year.
- The Park offers approximately 500 free public programs.
- Millennium Park was officially opened on July 16, 2004. The event lasted for 3 days. It was full of concerts and fun activities. Thousands of visitors came to celebrate the opening of the park.

18

Chicago Food

Chicago is popular for its fantastic restaurants and delicious food! You will find many food festivals, more than 8,000 restaurants, and many food trucks to satisfy you in Chicago. Its culinary scene has been featured in publications and magazines such as Bon Appetit and USA Today.

Some of Chicago's most iconic dishes are deep-dish pizza, the Chicago-style hotdog, and Garrett's popcorn.

Deep-Dish Pizza

Deep-dish pizza is one of Chicago's most iconic dishes of all time, with many people praising its delectable flavor and recipe.

Chicago Deep-Dish Pizza

Deep-dish pizza is a thick pizza that is layered with cheese, fillings like meat and vegetables, and sauce. The difference in Chicago deep-dish pizza is that the fillings are between two layers of crust and the sauce is on the top. Also, the deep-dish pizza's crust is so thick that it looks like a pie.

It is undecided who invented the recipe for Chicago-style deep-dish pizza, but some people credit Ike Sewell and Ric Riccardo at their restaurant Pizzeria Uno, popularizing it in the 1940s.

Chicago-Style Hotdog

The Chicago-style hotdog is one of Chicago's signature dishes that has captured the hearts of visitors and food lovers alike.

The Chicago-style hotdog is an all-beef dish that consists of a grilled or steamed sausage served in the slit of a poppy seed bun with yellow mustard, bright green sweet pickle relish, chopped white onions, a pickle spear, tomato slices, and celery salt as toppings.

Chicago Hotdog

The Chicago hotdog was introduced during the Great Depression (a period of the worldwide economic downturn during the 1930s) and made its way from Vienna to Chicago via Frankfurt. After arriving in Chicago, franks in buns became popular at fairs and baseball games.

Garrett's Popcorn

Garrett's Popcorn is one of the most notable popcorn stores. It originated in Chicago in 1949, introducing Chicago's original gourmet popcorn mix to people all over the world. Some of the first flavors sold at Garrett's Popcorn are Cheese Corn, Caramel Crisp, Buttery, and Plain.

The Chicago-style popcorn is a combination of caramel and cheese popcorn which Garrett's Popcorn made popular. It was then sold as Chicago Mix and handed across generations.

Garrett's Popcorn cooks delicious popcorn in small batches using natural ingredients and no preservatives. This popcorn shop has been in the gourmet popcorn industry for more than 70 years and is still patronized by customers.

Garrett's Popcorn

Chicago-Style Barbecue

Chicago-style barbecue is as sophisticated as Chicago itself. Chicago barbecue has different styles such as smokeless roast and Delta-style rib tips.

According to food historian Peter Engler, the first known barbecue restaurant in Chicago dates back to the 1930s. As millions of African Americans moved from the Mississippi Delta, a new barbecue style was developed that was distinguished by rapidly smoking meats over direct heat and then covering them with sweet sauce.

Eastern European immigrants also settled in the North Side of Chicago, bringing their love of boiled meats and sausages with them. Combining the two immigrant cooking styles, Chicago's signature barbecue menu was created.

Chicago-style barbecue is made by boiling and smoking ribs then adding the sauce. The rib tip combo is served with sauce, white bread, sausage, and French fries.

Brownies

Did you know that the first brownies were invented in Chicago?

The first brownie was created by chefs at Chicago's Palmer House Kitchen in the late 19th century at the direction of Bertha Palmer for the Columbian Exposition World's Fair in 1893.

The brownies are fudgy and sweet, with walnuts and an apricot glaze on top. The baked treat was an instant hit, despite not being given the name "brownie" right away, and it is still popular today.

You can indulge in a decadent taste of history baked especially for you at the Palmer House's pastry shop.

19

Chicago Sports

The city of Chicago is home to many successful sports teams and stadiums. It is one of four U.S. cities represented in all major American professional team sports (hockey, baseball, football, and soccer). Chicago is one of the best cities to see sports in the U.S.

The following is a little information about the sports fields in Chicago and the sports teams that call them home.

Guaranteed Rate Field

This baseball park is the home field of the Chicago White Sox. First opened in 1991, this field replaced Comiskey Park. The name then changed to "New Comiskey Park" in honor of the previous stadium. The White Sox made a new deal with the mortgage lender Guaranteed Rate in 2016, and that's the name the stadium has kept until now.

Guaranteed Rate Field is located on the south side of Chicago. It is across 35th St. From the original Comiskey Park. There are memories of the old field in the new park. For instance, the old park's home plate is memorialized by a marble plaque on the sidewalk. Foul lines from the old field are painted on the parking lot that is now located there.

Chicago White Sox - Baseball

The Chicago White Sox were originally named the White Stockings when they became a Major League Baseball team in 1900. The team was originally the St. Paul Saints when it was purchased by Charles Comiskey in 1894. The name White Stockings was soon shortened to the White Sox. The White Sox are an American League Central Division member of Major League Baseball.

Soldier Field

Constructed in 1924, Soldier Field is one of the few National Football League fields left that was built in the 1900s. Soldier is the home field of the

Chicago Bears Football Team and the Chicago Fire FC Soccer Team.

Soldier Field got its name from one of the greatest football games ever played. The game was played between the Army and Navy and ended in a tie, 21 to 21.

Soldier Field

Chicago Fire Soccer Club - Soccer

This team gets its name from the Great Chicago Fire of 1871. The Chicago Fire Soccer Club started on the 126th anniversary of the fire in 1997.

In 1998, the Chicago Fire won both the MLS (Major League Soccer) Cup and the U.S Open Cup in their first season.

Chicago Fire's colors are gold, red, and blue. The team played their games at the SeatGeek Stadium from 2006 - 2019, but have now moved back to Soldier Field (previously there in 2003 - 2005).

Chicago Bears - Football

The Chicago Bears Football team was founded in 1920. In 1921, they began playing in Chicago. The team used Wrigley Field as their home field through 1970, now playing at Soldier Field.

There are only five games in NFL history where the score was 2-0, and the Chicago Bears were in two of them. The first game was a loss for the Bears when they went against the Green Bay Packers in 1932. The second game resulted in a win for them against those same Packers. The team has a rivalry that is longstanding with the Packers.

United Center

United Center is an indoor arena that is home to the Chicago Bulls (basketball) and the Chicago Blackhawks (hockey).

The center is named for its sponsor, United Airlines. It is also one of the largest arenas by capacity in the National Basketball Association (NBA). It is also one of the largest arenas in the National Hockey League (NHL).

Currently, the arena is home to statues of Blackhawk legends Bobby Hull and Stan Mikita and Bulls legend Michael Jordan.

Chicago Blackhawks - Hockey

Frederic McLaughlin formed the Blackhawks team in 1936. The Blackhawks got their name from a World War I army squad nicknamed the Blackhawk Division.

The Blackhawks are part of the "Original Six" - a group of hockey teams that were part of the NHL from 1942 to 1967.

Chicago Bulls - Basketball

Founded on January 16, 1966, the Bulls won the playoffs during their first season. Dick Klein named the Bulls for the Chicago Union Stockyards. That was a primary business in Chicago. The Bulls are also the first team to win more than 70 games in one season.

Bull's famous players Michael Jordan and Derrick Rose both have been awarded the NBA most valuable player award. The Bulls have famous rivalries with the Detroit Pistons, the Miami Heat, the Cleveland Cavaliers, and the New York Knicks.

Wrigley Field

Wrigley field was called Weeghman Park from 1914 to 1920 and Cubs Park from 1920 to 1926. The field has been home to the Chicago Cubs since 1916 and is one of the oldest and most recognizable Major League Baseball parks in the U.S. The park only took two months to complete.

Wrigley Field

Chicago Cubs - Baseball

The Cubs started playing in 1870. The cubs are a part of the National League Central Division of Major League Baseball. The Cubs were also once known as the White Stockings, using the name for a while before the White Sox did. The Cubs were founded in 1876 and renamed the Cubs in 1903.

They suffered through a long dry spell without winning a world series championship series for over 100 years. They have won the world series three times (playing in 11 series) to date - 1907, 1908, and 2016. The win in 2016 ended the world series winning drought!

The Cubs' mascot is a bear cub named Clark. Clark first appeared with the Cubs in 2014.

Wintrust Arena

Also called DePaul Arena or McCormick Place Events Center, Wintrust Arena is the home of the Chicago Sky, a women's basketball team. The arena can seat around 11,000.

Chicago Sky - WNBA (Women's National Basketball Association)

The Sky is a women's professional basketball team based in Rosemount. Founded in 2005, both Michael J. Alter and Margaret Stender own the team. The team has been successful, making playoff appearances in 2013 - 2016 and playing in the WNBA finals in 2014. The team won the WNBA championship in 2021, which was their first championship win.

SeatGeek Stadium

This stadium opened its doors on June 11, 2006, under the name Toyota Park. Now called SeatGeek, this outdoor arena is a soccer-specific stadium home to the Chicago Red Stars. It is also the home stadium of the Chicago State Cougars men's and women's teams.

The stadium can seat around 20,000 people.

Chicago Red Stars - NWSL (National Women's Soccer League)

The Chicago Red Stars were a founding member of the NWSL and have played in that league since 2013. The team originally played in the WPS (Women's Professional Soccer) and the WPSL (Women's Premier Soccer League). The Red Stars hold the longest active playoff streak record (2015 - 2021) in the NWSL.

20

Chicago Walking and Bike Tours

One of the best ways to truly see a city is by walking or biking through it. Chicago offers many tours to help you better explore the city and its charm. Chicago tour companies offer a variety of tours to help you take in a lot of the most popular sights.

Here are a couple of tour companies and a little about each if the tours they offer.

Bobby's Bike Hike Chicago

Bobby's Bike Hike is one of the top-rated tour companies in Chicago. They offer walking tours to help tourists get oriented to the city as well as food tours, special holiday tours, and a comedy craft beer tour. Bobby's tour guides are true ambassadors of Chicago. A popular walking and food tour is the Chicago Favorites Walking and Food Tour, featuring classic Chicago food samples and a walk along the Chicago Riverwalk and Millennium Park.

Bobby's also offers bike tours for a variety of interests and skill levels. On a bike tour, you will visit some of Chicago's popular neighborhoods and parks and some of the top Chicago attractions. One of Bobby's popular tours is Chicago's Ultimate City Bike Tour (also known as the "Chicago 101" tour) which features Lakefront Trail, Navy Pier, Chicago Riverwalk, Field Museum, Shedd Aquarium, Soldier Field, and Adler Planetarium just to name a few.

Free Chicago Walking Tours

Free Chicago Walking Tours is a company that offers "pay what you would like" as a pricing guideline for their tours. You decide what the tour is worth, and that is what you pay. All Free Chicago Walking Tours last about 2 hours, and the distance is no longer than 2 miles. The company offers tours such as the Millennium Park tour, the Riverwalk tour, the Chicago crime and gangster tour, the Loop interior building and history tour, and an Architecture tour.

Walk Chicago Tours

Walk Chicago offers a multitude of different walking tours. They offer tours of neighborhoods (Little Italy, Gold Coast, Pilsen, Chinatown, Lincoln Park), art tours, and architecture tours. All tours through Walk Chicago are private tours with your group only.

Bike and Roll Chicago

Bike and Roll offers bike and Segway tours throughout Chicago. They also offer a bike rental service with suggested rides if you want to ride on your own. Some of the bike tours offered are through different neighborhoods. Bike and Roll also offers night bike tours and a haunted bike tour. Many if the same tours are also offered as Segway tours.

I hope you enjoyed visiting Chicago. Now let's head west to visit San Francisco where we will learn about some of the largest trees on the planet and the iconic cable cars!

https://kid-friendly-family-vacations.com/booktour-visitsf

Sign up for my newsletter for all upcoming updates as well as some free gifts.

https://kid-friendly-family-vacations.com/chicagofun

Head east to visit New York City to find out about a building that looks like an iron and a beach amusement park a short subway ride from downtown Manhattan!

https://kid-friendly-family-vacations.com/booktour-visitnyc

Visit all the cities in the Hey Kids! Let's Visit series!

https://kid-friendly-family-vacations.com/booktour-series

Please leave a review to help others learn more about Chicago whether traveling or learning from home.

https://kid-friendly-family-vacations.com/review-chicago

MORE FROM KID FRIENDLY FAMILY VACATIONS

BOOKS

Books to help build your kids / grandkids life experiences through travel and learning

https://kid-friendly-family-vacations.com/books

COLORING AND ACTIVITY PAGKAGES

Coloring pages, activity books, printable travel journals, and more in our Etsy shop

https://kid-friendly-family-vacations.com/etsy

RESOURCES FOR TEACHERS

Resources for teachers on Teachers Pay Teachers

https://kid-friendly-family-vacations.com/tpt

It is our mission to help you build your children's and grand-children's life experiences through travel. Not just traveling with your kids... building their "Life Experiences"! Join our community here:

https://kid-friendly-family-vacations.com/join/

Acknowledgements

Proofreading / Editing

Katie Erickson – KatieEricksonEditing.com

Cover Photos

Chicago Skyline - © rudi1976 / Deposit Photos

Cloud Gate - Millennium Park - © GaudiLab / Deposit Photos

Chicago-style deep-dish pizza - © bhofack2 / Deposit Photos

Soldier Field - © felixtm / Deposit Photos

Photos in Book

Art Institute of Chicago - Lion - © lokki61099 / Deposit Photos

Chicago Cultural Center - © rabbit75_dep / Deposit Photos

Harold Washington Library - © elesi / Deposit Photos

Chicago Lakefront Trail - © fotoluminate / Deposit Photos

Chicago Skyline - © rudi1976 / Deposit Photos

Maggie Daley Park - © sgoodwin4813 / Deposit Photos

Willis Tower Skydeck - © alekseigl / Deposit Photos

Hancock 360 Chicago Observatory - © vaneveval / Deposit Photos

Tribune Tower - © jekershner7 / Deposit Photos

Grant Park - © starmaro / Deposit Photos

Adler Planetarium - © benkrut / Deposit Photos

Shedd Aquarium - © benkrut / Deposit Photos

Field Museum - © benkrut / Deposit Photos

Chicago Riverwalk - © steveheap / Deposit Photos

Chicago River - © jirabu / Deposit Photos

Navy Pier - © AKDREAMS / Deposit Photos

Grant Park Conservatory - © benkrut / Deposit Photos

Museum of Science and Industry - © benkrut / Deposit Photos

Lincoln Park Zoo – Jay Pritzker Pavilion © bennnn@hotmail.com / Deposit Photos

Millennium Park - © lokki61099 / Deposit Photos

Cloud Gate - Millennium Park - © GaudiLab / Deposit Photos

Cloud Gate - Millennium park - with reflection - © Indigo Luna

Chicago-style deep-dish pizza - © bhofack2 / Deposit Photos

Chicago-style hotdog - © bhofack2 / Deposit Photos

Garrett's popcorn - © bhofack2 / Deposit Photos

Soldier Field - © felixtm / Deposit Photos

Wrigley Field - personal vacation photo

About the Author

Teresa Mills is the bestselling author of the "Hey Kids! Let's Visit..." Book Series for Kids!

Teresa's goal through her books and website is to help parents / grandparents who want to build the life experiences of their children / grandchildren through travel and learning activities.

She is an active mother and Mimi. She and her family love traveling in the USA, and internationally too! They love exploring new places, eating cool foods, and having yet another adventure as a family! With the Mills, it's all about traveling as family.

In addition to traveling, Teresa enjoys reading, hiking, biking, and helping others.

Join in the fun at kid-friendly-family-vacations.com

Made in the USA
Monee, IL
11 September 2023